FINGERPICKING
standards

HLE

HAL LEONARD EUROPE
Distributed by Music Sales

Exclusive Distributors:
Music Sales Limited
14–15 Berners Street, London W1T 3LJ, UK.

Order No. HLE90002693
ISBN 1-84609-355-4
This book © Copyright 2006 by Hal Leonard Europe

Cover design by Fresh Lemon
Printed in the USA

www.musicsales.com

Your Guarantee of Quality
As publishers, we strive to produce every
book to the highest commercial standards.
The book has been carefully designed
to minimise awkward page turns and to
make playing from it a real pleasure.
Throughout, the printing and binding
have been planned to ensure a sturdy,
attractive publication which should
give years of enjoyment.
If your copy fails to meet our high
standards, please inform us and we
will gladly replace it.

INTRODUCTION TO FINGERSTYLE GUITAR 5

CAN'T HELP FALLING IN LOVE 6

CRAZY 12

FLY ME TO THE MOON (IN OTHER WORDS) 9

GEORGIA ON MY MIND 16

I COULD WRITE A BOOK 18

LOVE ME TENDER 20

MISTY 26

MOON RIVER 28

MY FAVORITE THINGS 23

UNCHAINED MELODY 30

WHAT A WONDERFUL WORLD 33

WHEN I FALL IN LOVE 36

YESTERDAY 38

YOU ARE MY SUNSHINE 41

YOU ARE SO BEAUTIFUL 44

INTRODUCTION TO FINGERSTYLE GUITAR

Fingerstyle (a.k.a. fingerpicking) is a guitar technique that means you literally pick the strings with your right-hand fingers and thumb. This contrasts with the conventional technique of strumming and playing single notes with a pick (a.k.a. flatpicking). For fingerpicking, you can use any type of guitar: acoustic steel-string, nylon-string classical, or electric.

THE RIGHT HAND

The most common right-hand position is shown below:

Use a high wrist; arch your palm as if you were holding a ping-pong ball. Keep the thumb outside and away from the fingers, and let the fingers do the work rather than lifting your whole hand.

The thumb generally plucks the bottom strings with downstrokes on the left side of the thumb and thumbnail. The other fingers pluck the higher strings using upstokes with the fleshy tip of the fingers and fingernails. The thumb and fingers should pluck one string per stroke and not brush over several strings.

Another picking option you may choose to use is called **hybrid picking** (a.k.a. plectrum-style fingerpicking). Here, the pick is usually held between the thumb and first finger, and the three remaining fingers are assigned to pluck the higher strings.

THE LEFT HAND

The left-hand fingers are numbered 1 though 4:

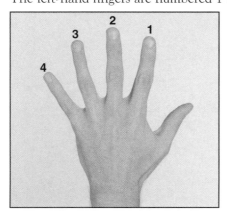

Be sure to keep your fingers arched, with each joint bent; if they flatten out across the strings, they will deaden the sound when you fingerpick. As a general rule, let the strings ring as long as possible when playing fingerstyle.

Can't Help Falling In Love

from the Paramount Picture BLUE HAWAII

Words and Music by George David Weiss, Hugo Peretti and Luigi Creatore

Intro
Moderately slow

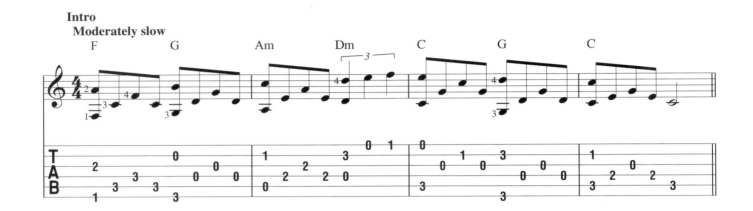

Verse

1. Wise men say only fools rush in, but
2. Shall I stay? Would it be a sin, if

I can't help fall-ing in love with you.
I can't help fall-ing in love with you?

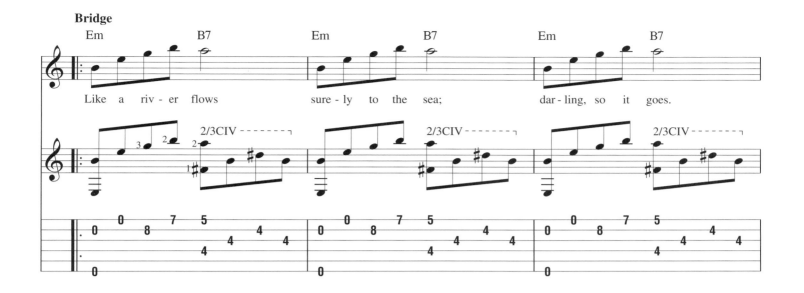

I can't help fall-ing in love with you.

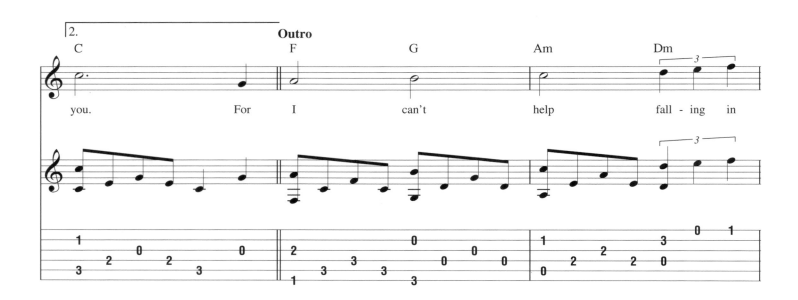

2.

Outro

you. For I can't help fall-ing in

love with you.

Fly Me To The Moon
(In Other Words)

featured in the Motion Picture ONCE AROUND

Words and Music by Bart Howard

In oth - er words, darl - ing kiss me.

Verse

2. Fill my heart with song ___ and let me sing for - ev - er

more. You are all I long for, all I

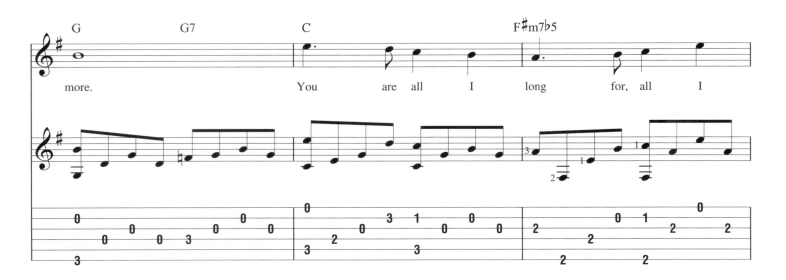

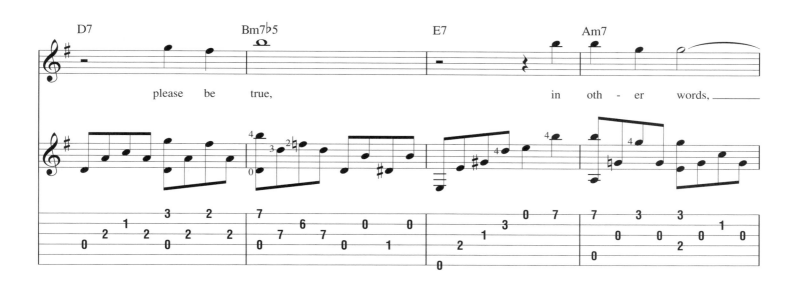

Crazy

Words and Music by Willie Nelson

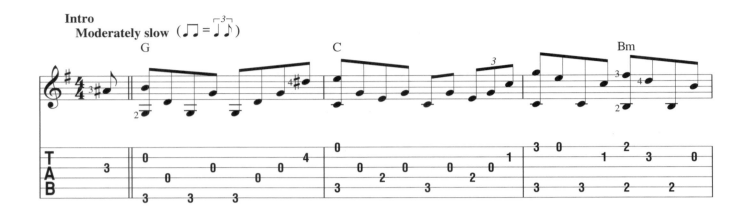

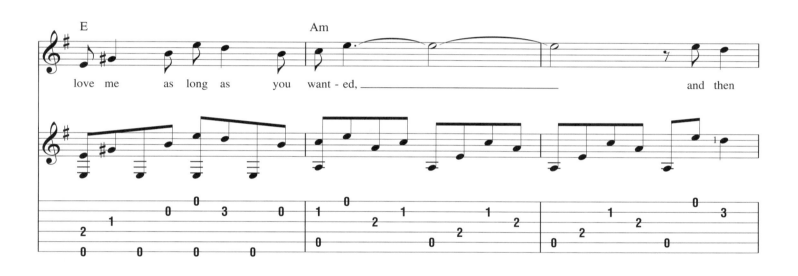

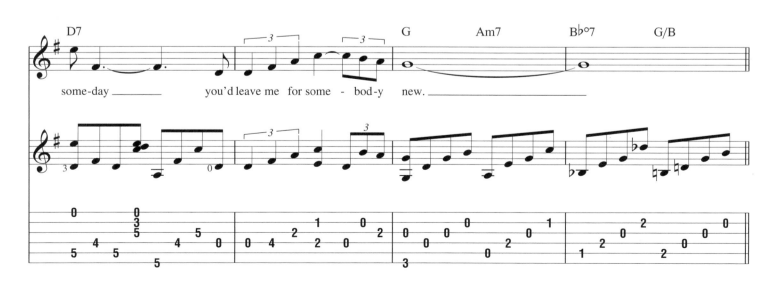

Bridge

Wor - ry, ___ why do I let my - self wor - ry, ___

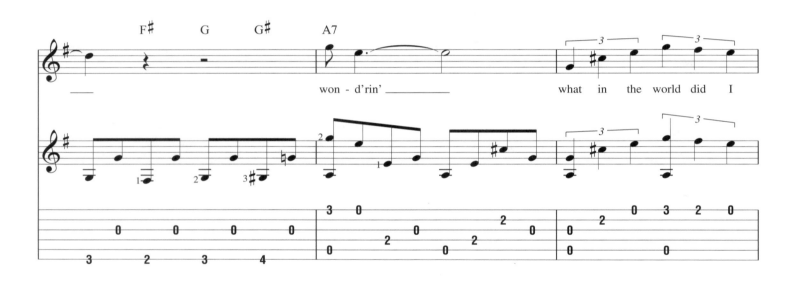

___ won - d'rin' ___ what in the world did I

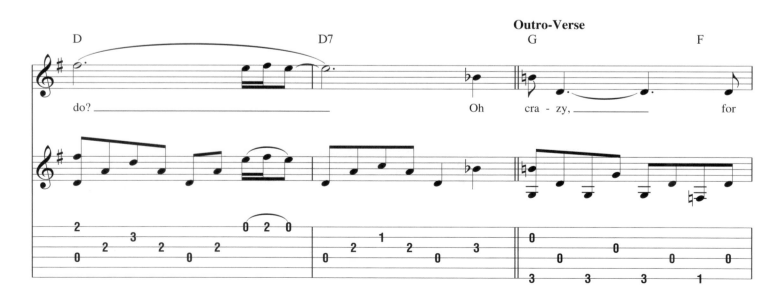

do? ___ Oh cra - zy, ___ for

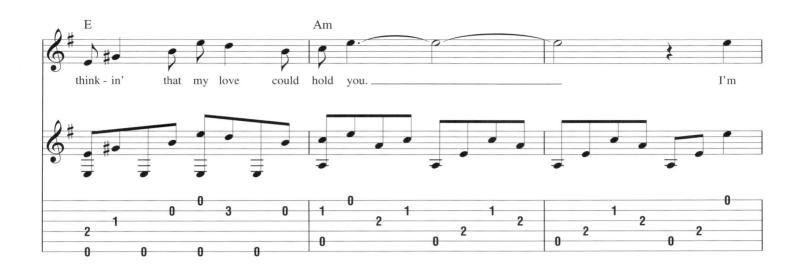

think - in' that my love could hold you. _____ I'm

cra - zy for try - in', and cra - zy for cry - in', ___ and I'm cra - zy for lov - in'

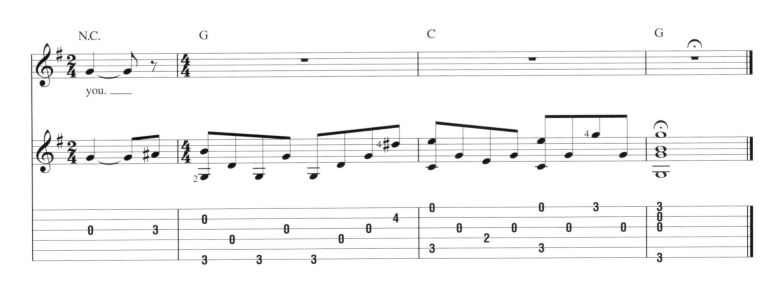

you. ___

Georgia On My Mind

Words by Stuart Gorrell
Music by Hoagy Carmichael

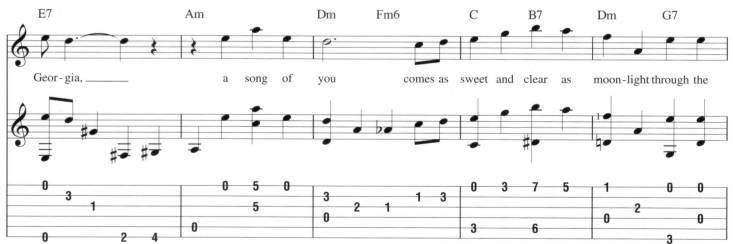

I Could Write A Book

from PAL JOEY

Words by Lorenz Hart
Music by Richard Rodgers

sim - ple se - cret of the plot _____ is just to tell them that I love you a

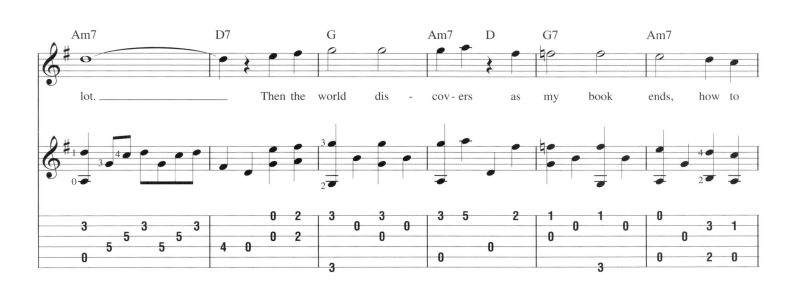

lot. _____ Then the world dis - cov - ers as my book ends, how to

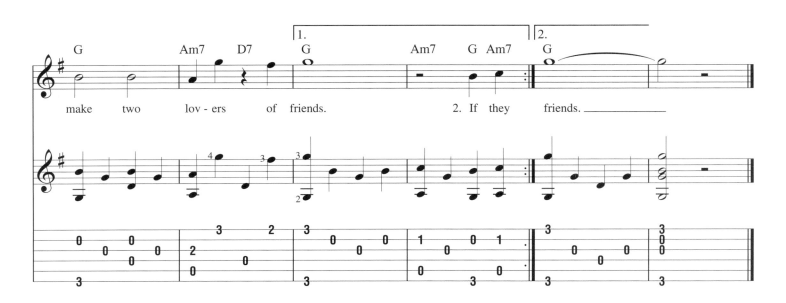

make two lov - ers of friends. 2. If they friends. _____

Love Me Tender

Words and Music by Elvis Presley and Vera Matson

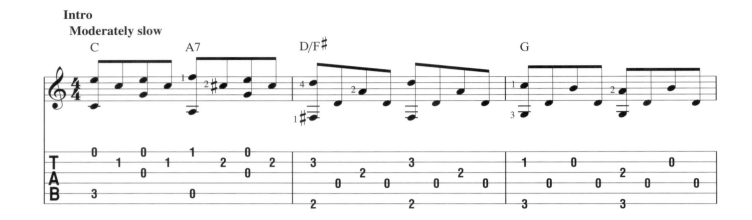

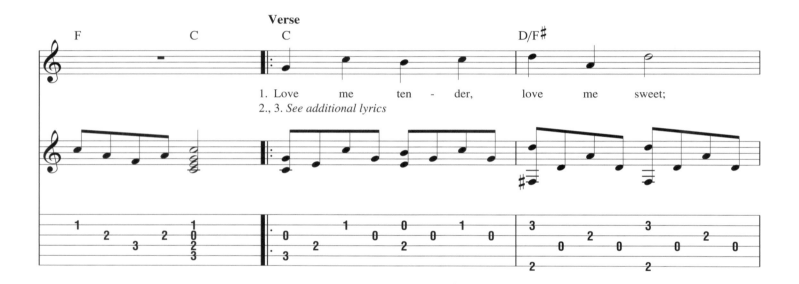

1. Love me ten - der, love me sweet;
2., 3. *See additional lyrics*

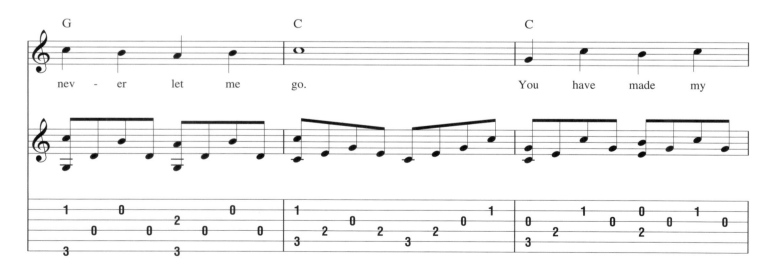

nev - er let me go. You have made my

Chorus

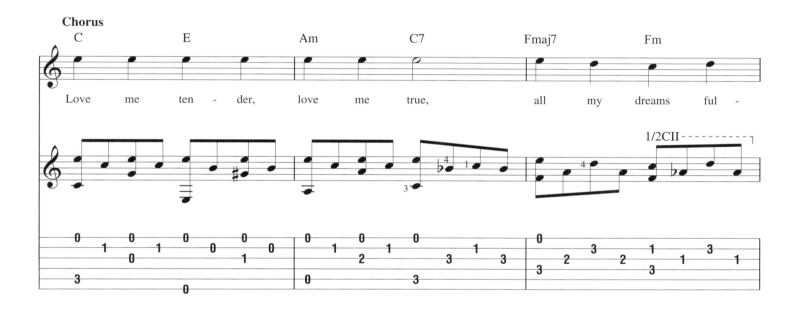

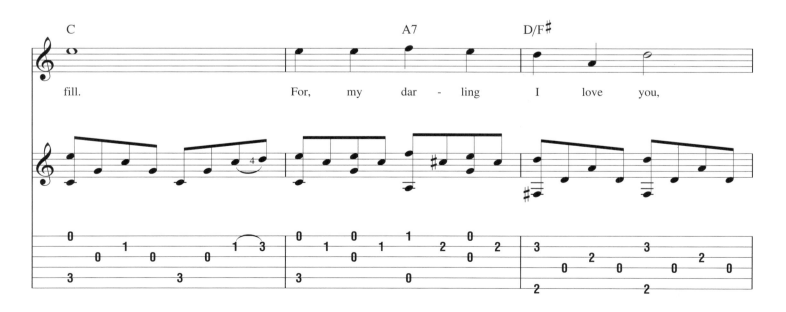

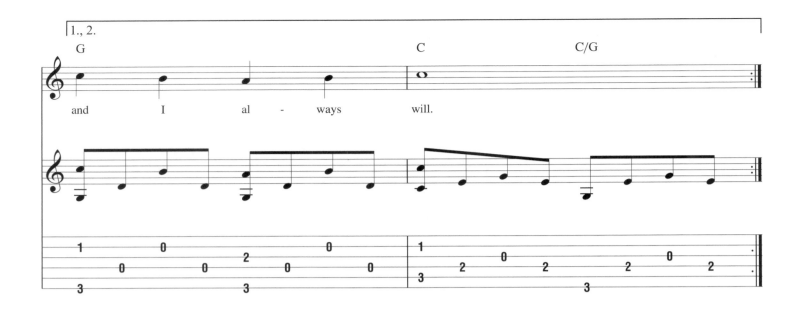

and   I   al - ways   will.

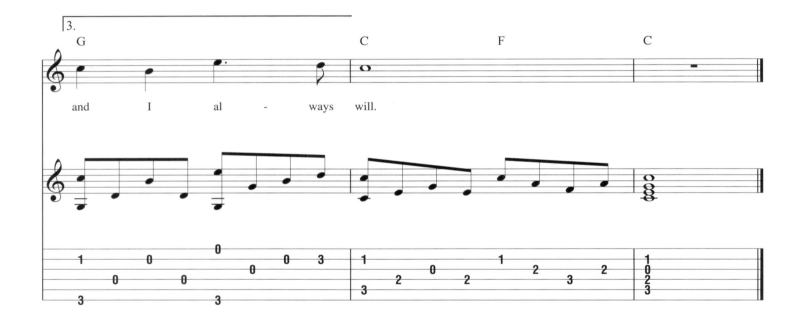

and   I   al - ways   will.

Additional Lyrics

2. Love me tender, love me long;
   Take me to your heart.
   For it's there that I belong,
   And we'll never part.

3. Love me tender, love me dear;
   Tell me you are mine.
   I'll be yours through all the years,
   Till the end of time.

My Favorite Things

from THE SOUND OF MUSIC

Lyrics by Oscar Hammerstein II
Music by Richard Rodgers

Verse

3. Girls in white dress-es with blue sat-in sash-es, snow-flakes that stay on my nose and eye-

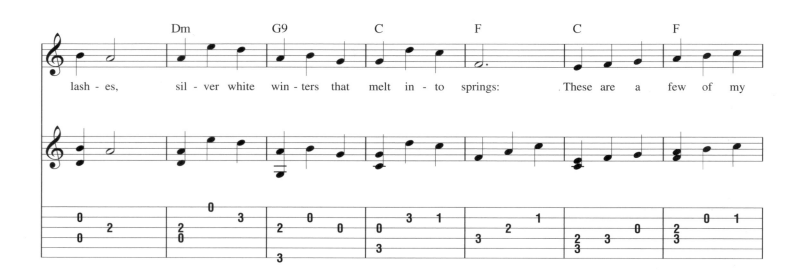

lash-es, sil-ver white win-ters that melt in-to springs: These are a few of my

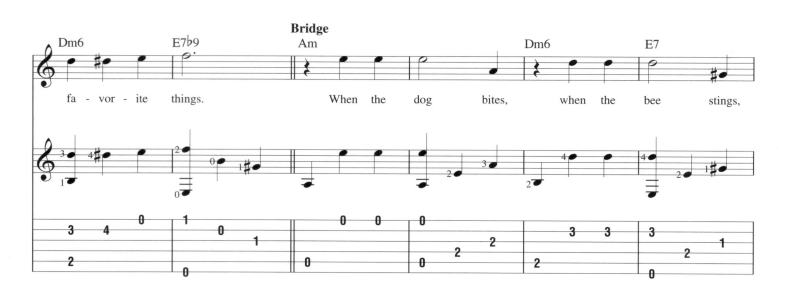

Bridge

fa-vor-ite things. When the dog bites, when the bee stings,

when I'm feel - ing sad, _____ I sim - ply re - mem - ber my

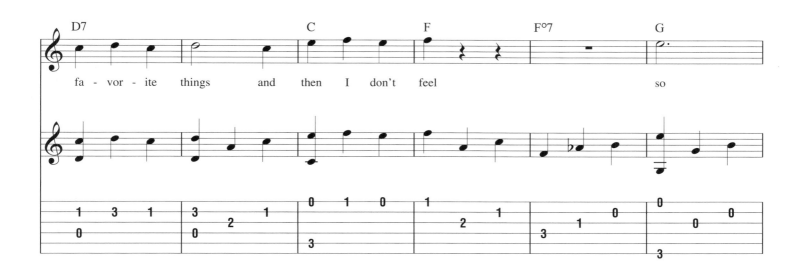

fa - vor - ite things and then I don't feel so

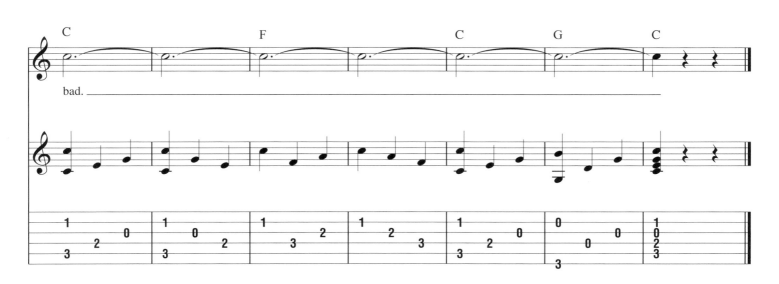

bad. _____

Misty

Words by Johnny Burke
Music by Erroll Garner

Additional Lyrics

2. Walk my way,
   And a thousand violins begin to play,
   Or it might be the sound of your hello,
   That music I hear,
   I get misty the moment you're near.

3. On my own,
   Would I wander through this wonderland alone,
   Never knowing my right foot from my left,
   My hat from my glove?
   I'm too misty and too much in love.

Moon River

from the Paramount Picture BREAKFAST AT TIFFANY'S

Words by Johnny Mercer
Music by Henry Mancini

Unchained Melody

from the Motion Picture UNCHAINED

Lyric by Hy Zaret
Music by Alex North

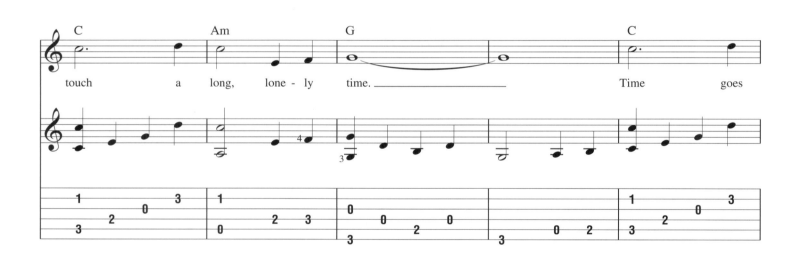

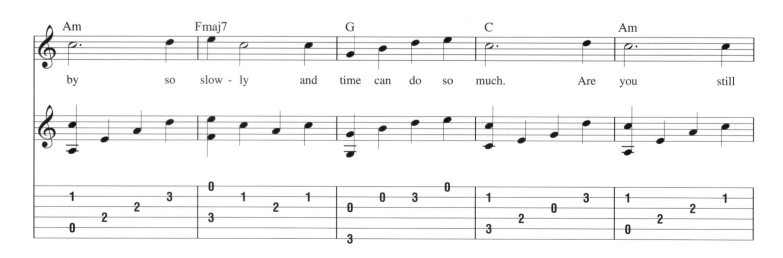

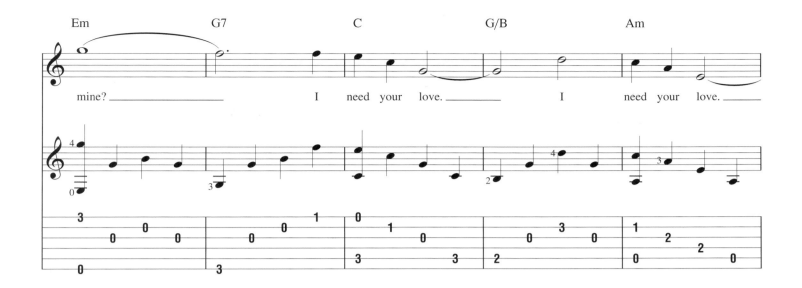

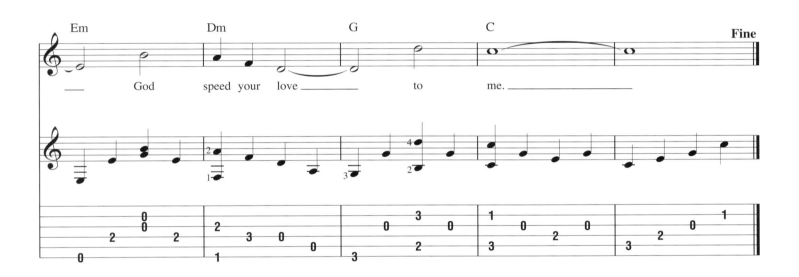

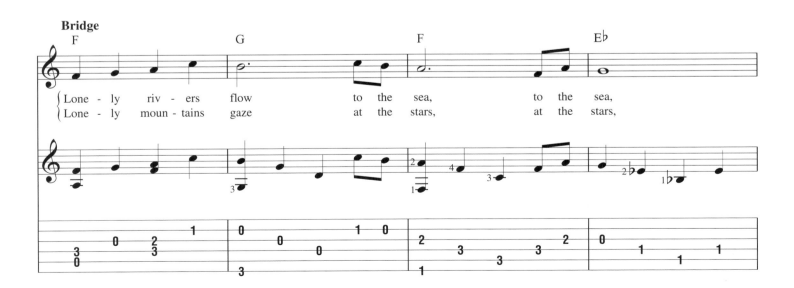

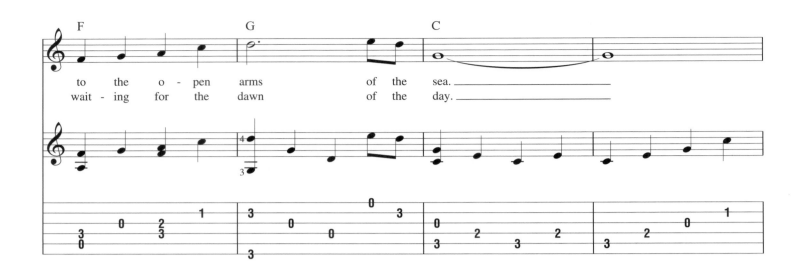

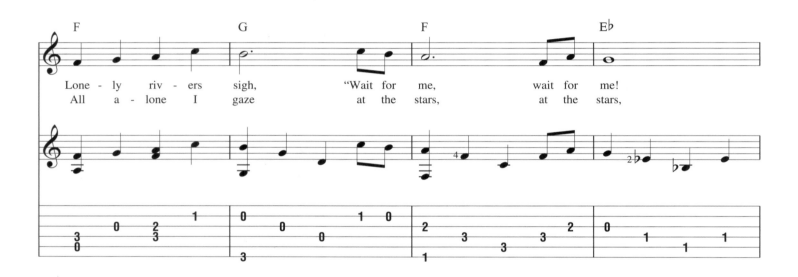

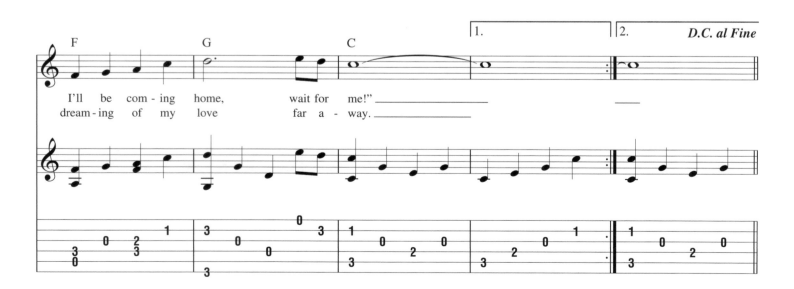

What A Wonderful World

Words and Music by George David Weiss and Bob Thiele

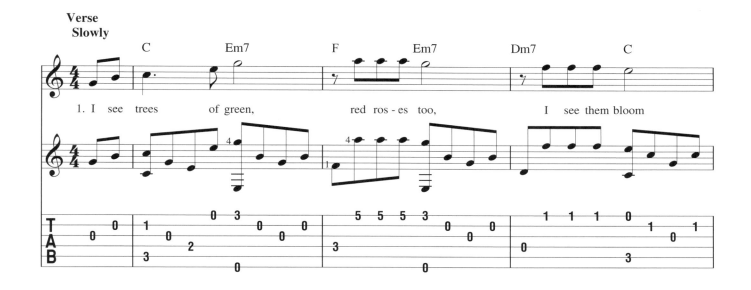

1. I see trees of green, red ros-es too, I see them bloom

for me and you, and I think to my-self, what a won-der-ful world.

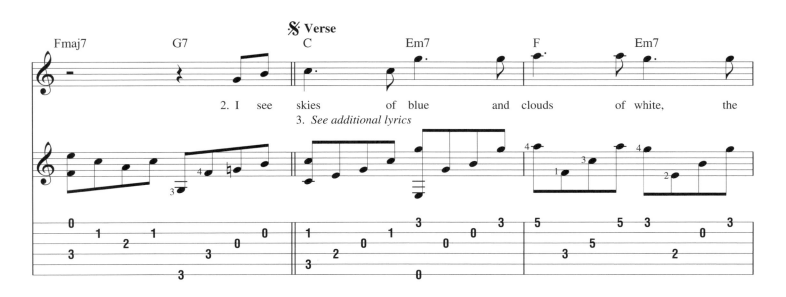

2. I see skies of blue and clouds of white, the
3. *See additional lyrics*

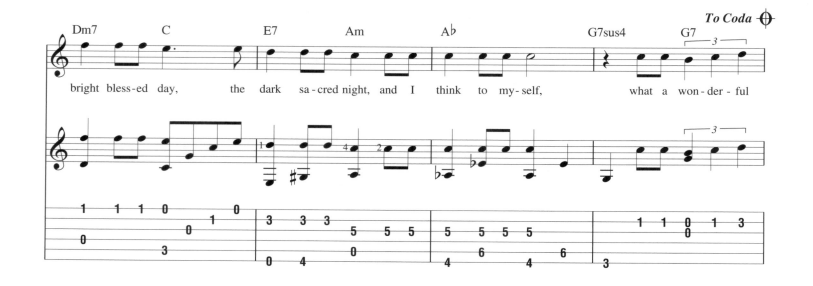

bright bless-ed day, the dark sa-cred night, and I think to my-self, what a won-der-ful

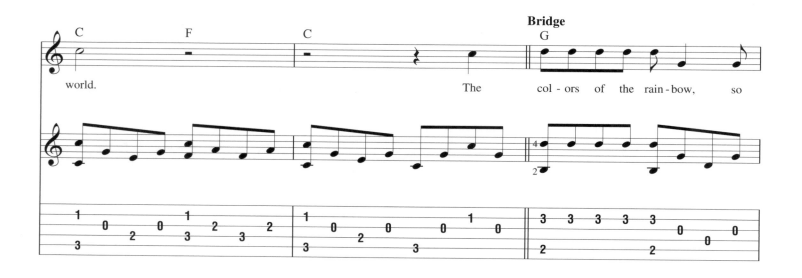

world. The col-ors of the rain-bow, so

Bridge

pret-ty in the sky are al-so on the fac-es of peo-ple go-in' by. I see

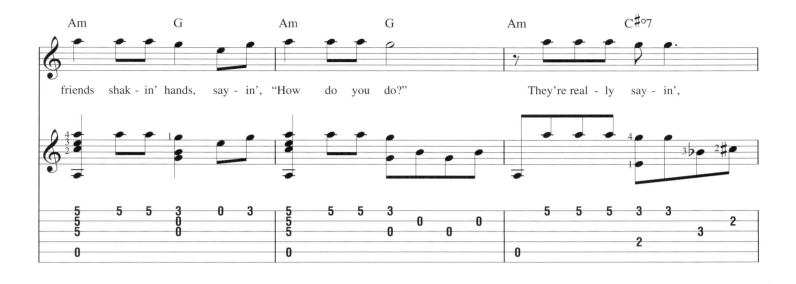

friends shak-in' hands, say-in', "How do you do?" They're real-ly say-in',

Coda

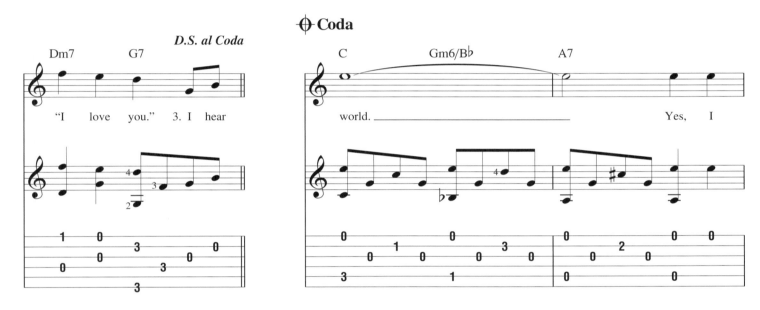

D.S. al Coda

"I love you." 3. I hear

world. _____ Yes, I

think to my-self what a won-der-ful world.

Additional Lyrics

3. I hear babies cry, I watch them grow;
They'll learn much more than I'll ever know.
And I think to myself, what a wonderful world.
Yes, I think to myself, what a wonderful world.

When I Fall In Love

Words by Edward Heyman
Music by Victor Young

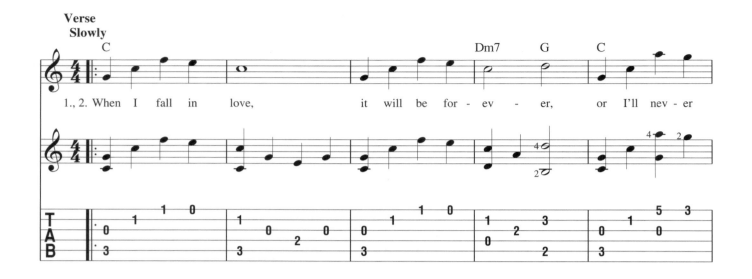

1., 2. When I fall in love, it will be for- ev- er, or I'll nev- er

fall in love. _____ In a rest- less world like this is, love is

end- ed be- fore it's be- gun, and too man- y moon- light kiss- es seem to

Yesterday

Words and Music by John Lennon and Paul McCartney

Bridge

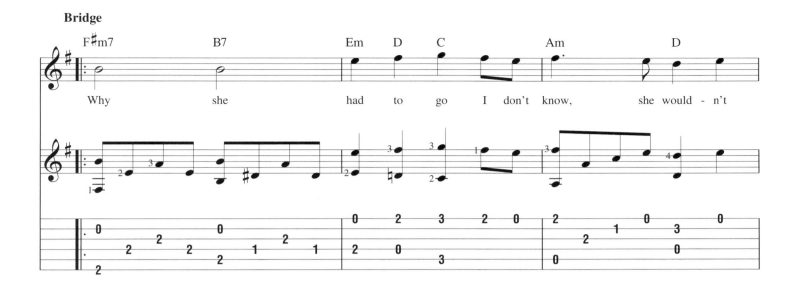

Why she had to go I don't know, she would-n't

say. I said some-thing wrong, now I

Verse

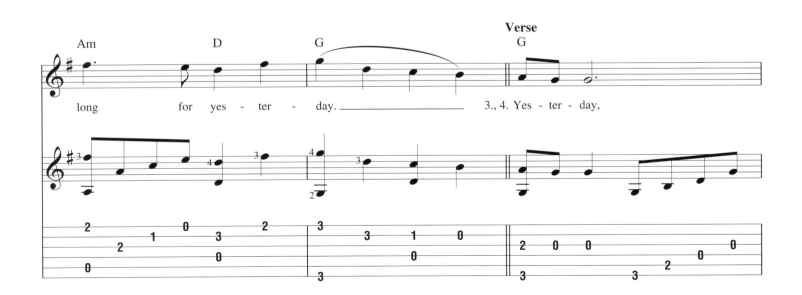

long for yes-ter-day. _____ 3., 4. Yes-ter-day,

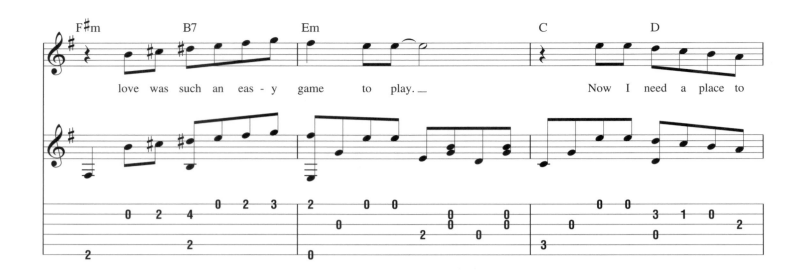

love was such an eas-y game to play. — Now I need a place to

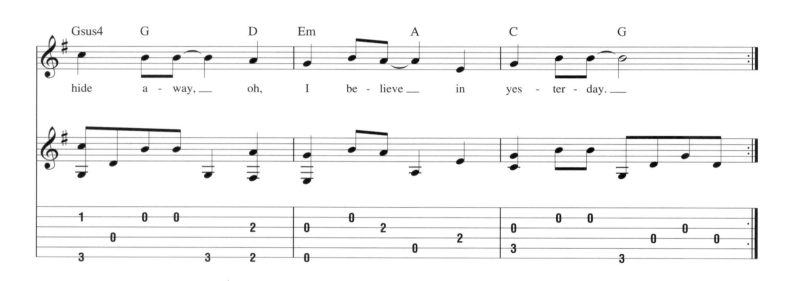

hide a - way, — oh, I be - lieve — in yes - ter - day. —

Outro

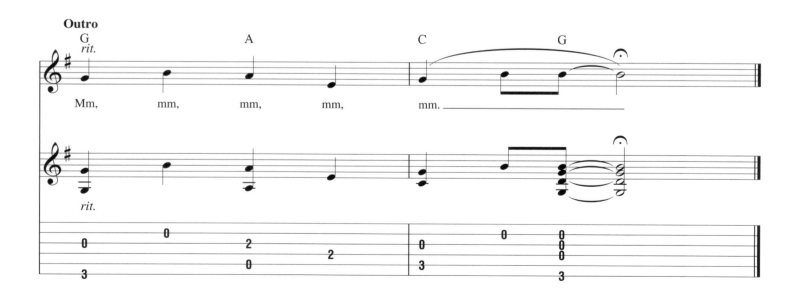

Mm, mm, mm, mm, mm. _____

You Are My Sunshine

Words and Music by Jimmie Davis

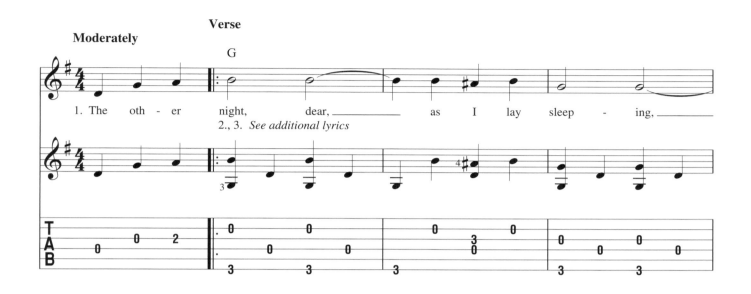

1. The oth - er night, dear, ___ as I lay sleep - ing, ___
2., 3. *See additional lyrics*

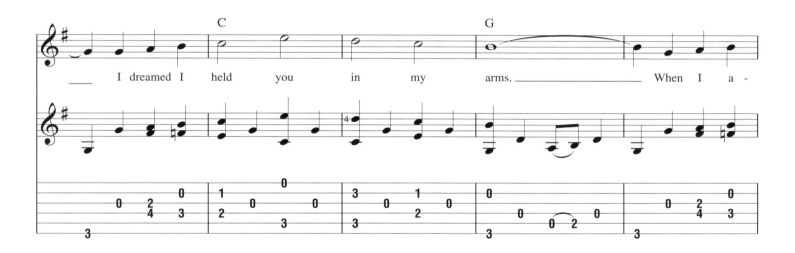

___ I dreamed I held you in my arms. ___ When I a -

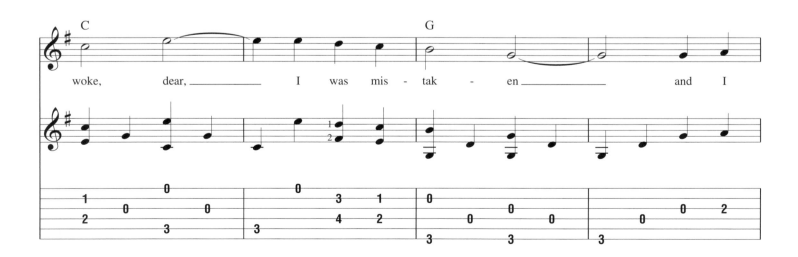

woke, dear, ___ I was mis - tak - en ___ and I

Chorus

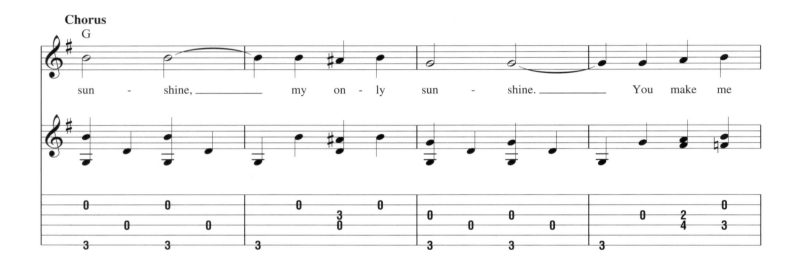

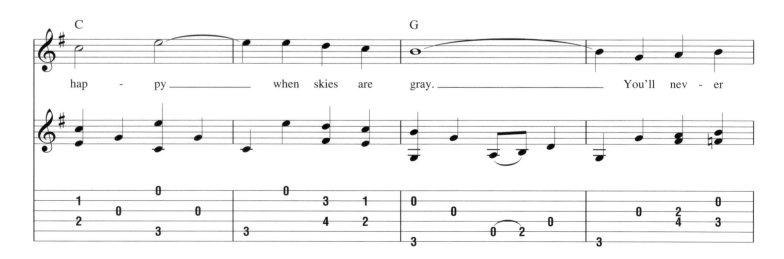

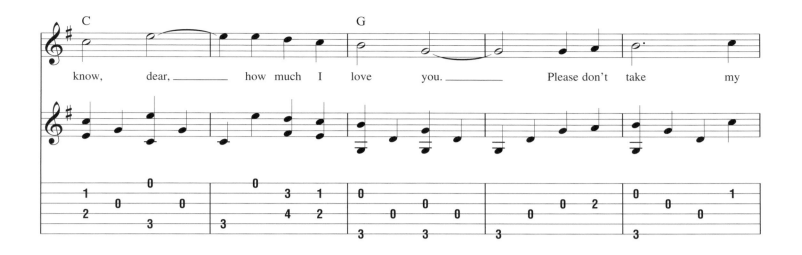

know, dear, _____ how much I love you. _____ Please don't take my

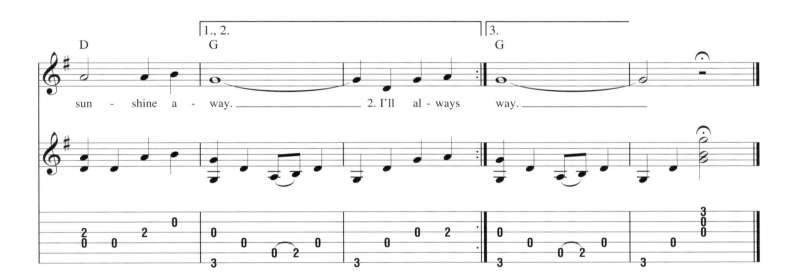

sun - shine a - way. _____ 2. I'll al - ways way. _____

Additional Lyrics

2. I'll always love you and make you happy
   If you will only say the same.
   But if you leave me to love another,
   You'll regret it all some day.

3. You told me once, dear, you really loved me
   And no one else could come between.
   But now you've left me and love another;
   You have shattered all my dreams.

You Are So Beautiful

Words and Music by Billy Preston and Bruce Fisher

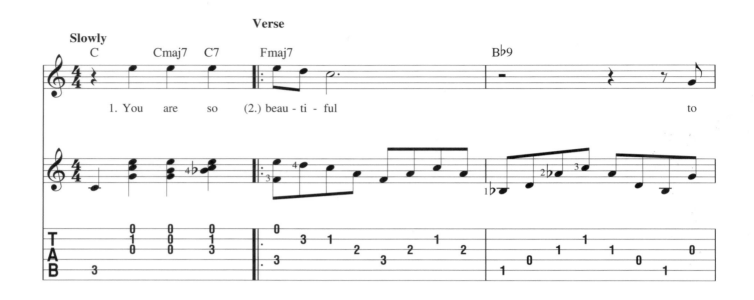

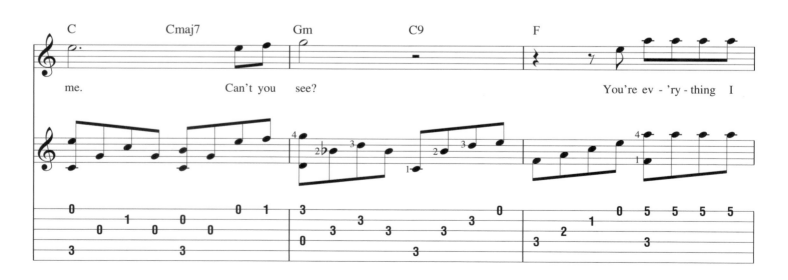